Book 1

YOU'RE IN THE BAND

T0069848

For Lead Guitar
by Dave Clo

Includes Online Audio

Speed • Pitch • Balance • Loop

Each song includes two audio tracks: one at a manageable rehearsal tempo, and the other at a faster performance tempo.
With our exclusive **PLAYBACK+** feature, you can change the tempo even more without altering the pitch,
plus set loop points for continuous repetition of tricky measures.

To access audio, visit:
www.halleonard.com/mylibrary

Enter Code
7439-1725-7856-8414

Recording Musicians:
DAVE CLO – Guitars and Bass
TIM CLO – Drums

Cover Photograph by Mike Gillespie
Garage used by permission of Richard and Alma Finke
Adplate photos used by permission of **jj@astartledchameleon.co.uk**

ISBN 978-0-87718-002-9

WILLIS MUSIC

EXCLUSIVELY DISTRIBUTED BY

HAL•LEONARD®
7777 W. BLUEMOUND RD. P.O. BOX 13819
MILWAUKEE, WISCONSIN 53213

Visit Hal Leonard Online at
www.halleonard.com

2   **Congratulations!** We've talked it over and decided that "You're In the Band!"

Here is a list of the songs you will need to learn. When you can play your part with the rehearsal track without any mistakes, write the date mastered to the right of the rehearsal track space. When you have perfected a song with the performance track, write in that date too. GET BUSY! We have our first show in about six months!

🔊   Whenever this icon appears, that means that there are audio tracks that you can stream or download online using the special code on the first page.

SONG INDEX

Page	Title	Date Rehearsal Track Mastered	Date Performance Track Mastered
6	Rock-E		
7	Grunge-E		
8	Effigy		
9	E-Mail		
10	Two Down		
11	Besieged		
12	2nd Stringer		
13	Phrygian Sea		
14	The Gauge		
15	Ice Age		
16	Spare		
17	Graduation		
18	Geology		
20	Forthright?		
21	Delivery		
22	Staircase		
23	Pentatonic		
24	Adrian		
25	Out on a Ledger		
26	5th Wheel		
27	A Minor Setback		
28	Rock-E VI		
29	Surf String		
30	Octavee		
31	Upshot		

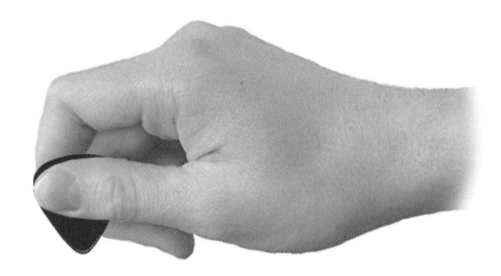

The pick should be held between the thumb and the index finger. Use only a downward motion when plucking the string until 8th notes are introduced on page 12.

WHAT'S THAT CALLED?

the body **the neck** **the head**

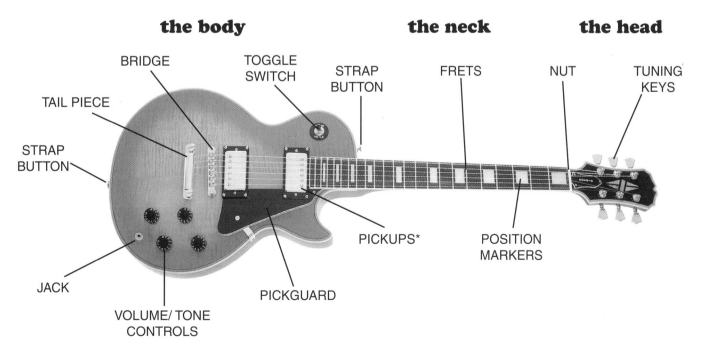

BRIDGE

TOGGLE SWITCH

STRAP BUTTON

FRETS

NUT

TUNING KEYS

TAIL PIECE

STRAP BUTTON

PICKUPS*

POSITION MARKERS

JACK

PICKGUARD

VOLUME/ TONE CONTROLS

*ACOUSTIC GUITARS HAVE A "SOUND HOLE" INSTEAD OF PICKUPS.

Tuning the guitar can be very difficult for a beginner, but it's an important first step. Tune your guitar with the tuning track online (or with a pitch pipe, tuning fork, piano, electronic tuner, or smartphone app). Do this at each practice session until you are ready to tune the guitar on your own. The tuning track online contains each string played 3 times, starting with the highest string (E – see string #1 below).

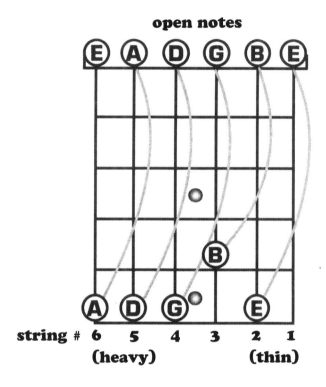

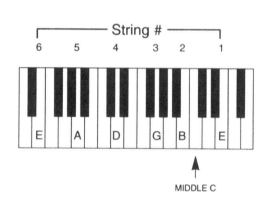

Once you are comfortable with the idea of tuning the guitar yourself, follow these steps:

1. **TUNE THE FIRST STRING OPEN (pluck the string without pressing any frets) TO AN "E". Use a pitch pipe, tuning fork, piano or any reliable source.**

2. **MATCH THE "E" ON THE 5th FRET OF THE 2nd STRING TO SOUND LIKE THE 1st STRING OPEN.**

3. **MATCH THE "B" ON THE 4th FRET OF THE 3rd STRING TO SOUND LIKE THE 2nd STRING OPEN.**

4. **MATCH THE "G" ON THE 5th FRET OF THE 4th STRING TO SOUND LIKE THE 3rd STRING OPEN.**

5. **MATCH THE "D" ON THE 5th FRET OF THE 5th STRING TO SOUND LIKE THE 4th STRING OPEN.**

6. **MATCH THE "A" ON THE 5th FRET OF THE 6th STRING TO SOUND LIKE THE 5th STRING OPEN.**

7. **PLAY YOUR GUITAR. IT SHOULD BE IN TUNE.**

THE BASICS

The **staff** -- made up of 5 lines

bar lines -- separate measures

measure 1   measure 2   measure 3   measure 4

treble clef -- the clef that is used when writing guitar music

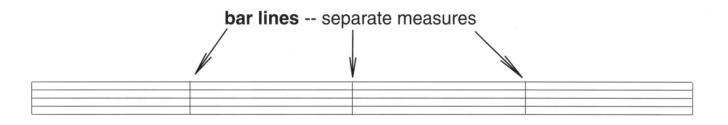

common time -- 4 beats per measure

whole note	half notes	quarter notes	8th notes
4 beats	2 beats	1 beat	2 for 1 beat

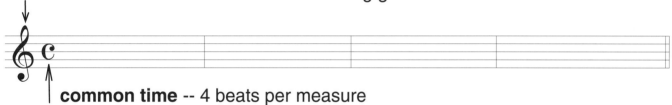

1 2 3 4   1 2 3 4   1 2 3 4   1 & 2 & 3 & 4 &

dotted half notes
3 beats

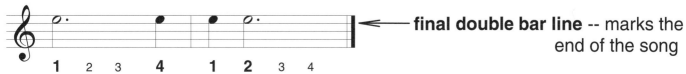

final double bar line -- marks the end of the song

1 2 3 4   1 2 3 4

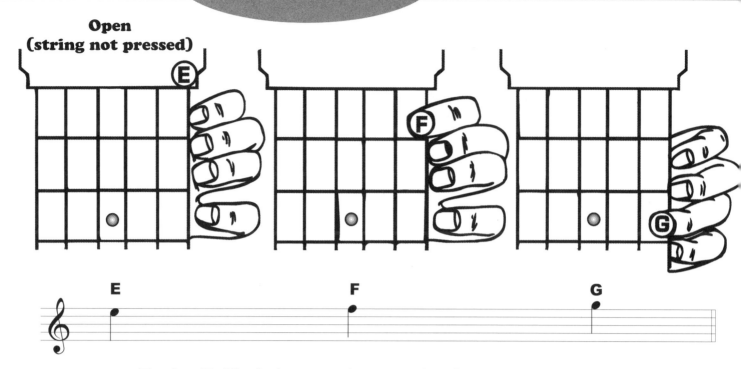

To play E: Pluck down on the 1st string (smallest string) open.*
To play F: Place the 1st finger (index) on the 1st fret of this string.**
To play G: Place the 3rd finger (ring) on the 3rd fret of this string.**

ROCK-E

Teacher's Chords

* Open means to pluck the string without pressing any frets.

** The term "on the fret" really means next to the fret as pictured.

GRUNG-E

PATTERNS TO RECOGNIZE

Learn to recognize notes in groups, the same way
we recognize words by grouping several letters.

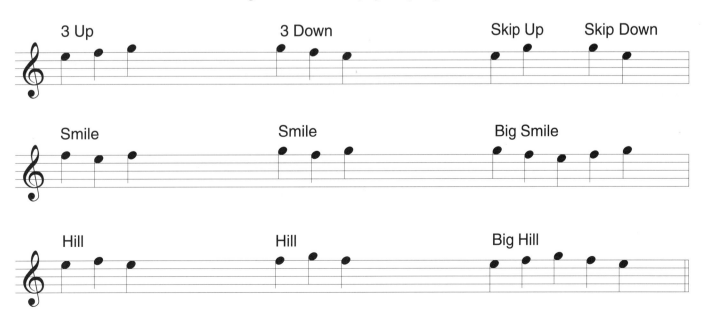

EFFIGY

Teacher's Notes

E-MAIL

MAKE SURE YOU'VE MASTERED ALL THE SONGS WITH E, F, AND G BEFORE ADVANCING TO THE NEXT STRING.

THE SECOND STRING B

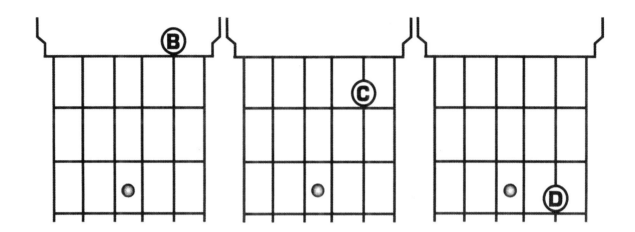

To play B: Pluck the 2nd string open.
To play C: Place the 1st finger on the 1st fret of this string.
To play D: Place the 3rd finger on the 3rd fret of this string.

TWO DOWN

BESIEGED

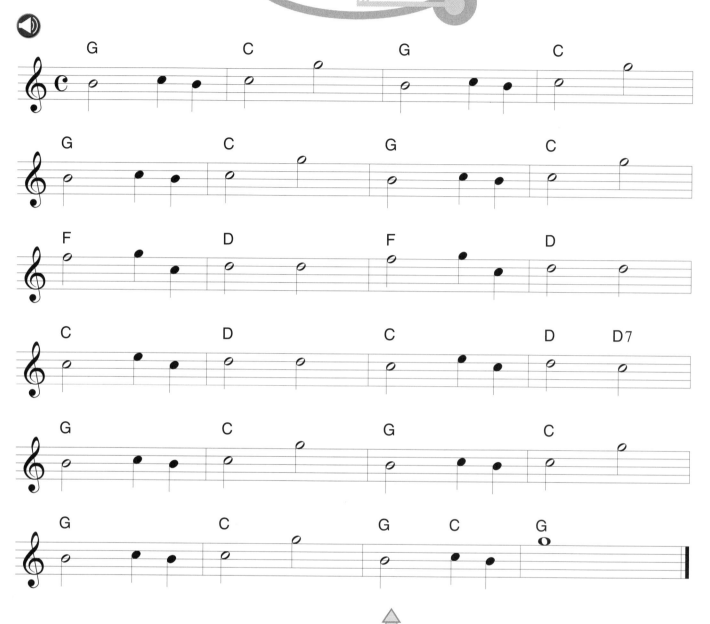

Notes

2ND STRINGER

Fact File

PLAYING EIGHTH NOTES

When playing eighth notes, your picking hand does not change speed.
The pick plucks down on the string (as usual) and also up on the string
on the way back. By plucking down and then up you will double the amount
of times the string is hit without increasing your hand speed.

⊓ **DOWN-PICK**

V **UP-PICK**

PHRYGIAN SEA

Shortcut:

If you are getting confused with the notes you have learned so far, here's the standard shortcut to recognizing all of the notes on the staff:

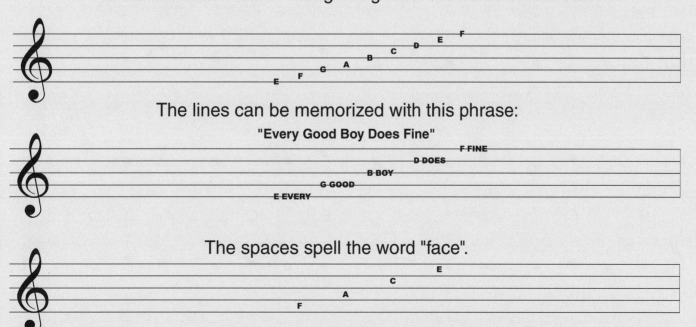

The lines can be memorized with this phrase:

"Every Good Boy Does Fine"

The spaces spell the word "face".

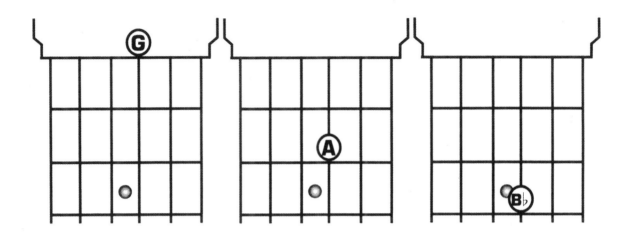

G   A   B flat

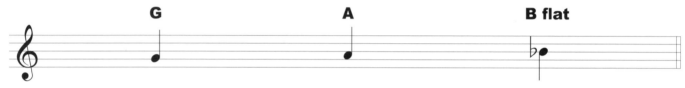

(not used until page 16)

To play G: Pluck the 3rd string open.
To play A: Place the 2nd finger on the 2nd fret of this string.
To play B♭ (B flat): Place the 3rd finger on the 3rd fret of this string.

THE GAUGE

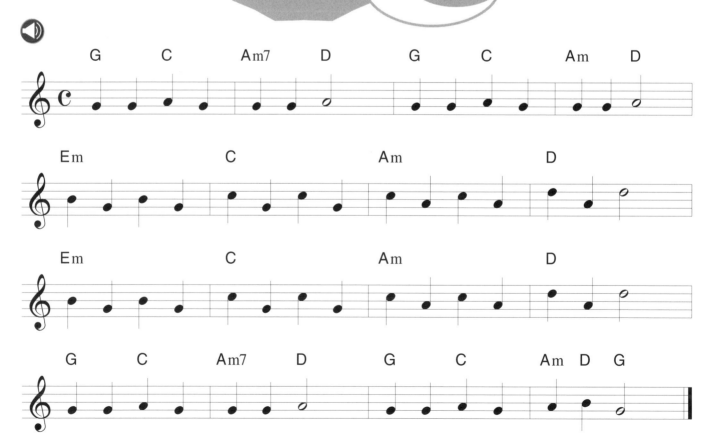

ICE AGE

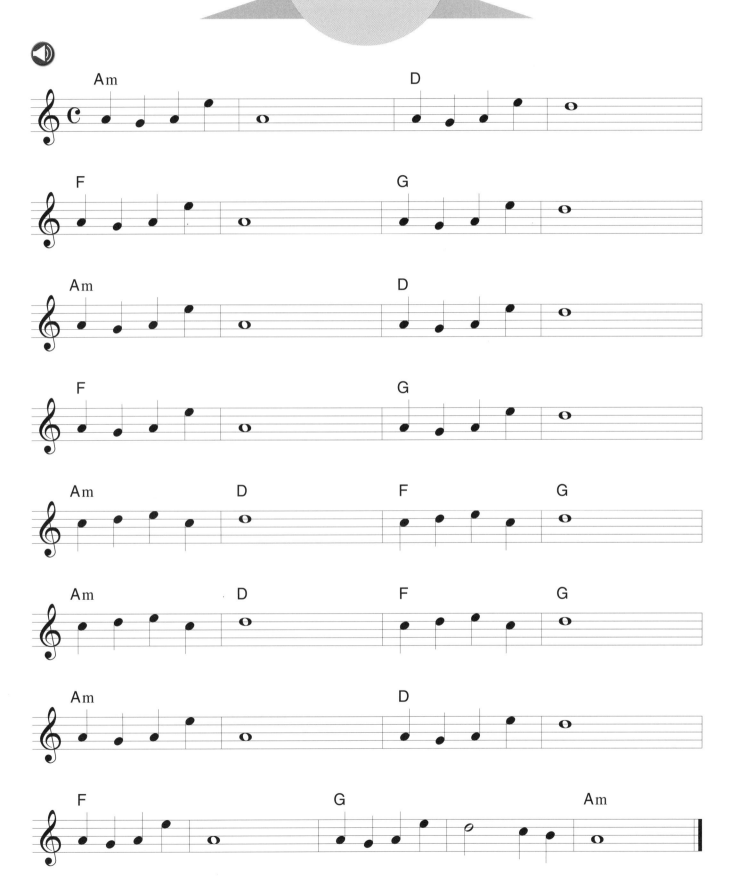

Fact File

TO "B" OR TO "B FLAT"

The flat symbol ♭ that is placed in front of a B note makes "B flat."
The symbol will only appear once in a measure to make all B's into B flats.
Once the measure is over, the flat is no longer in effect. The natural sign ♮
can be used to restore B within a measure.

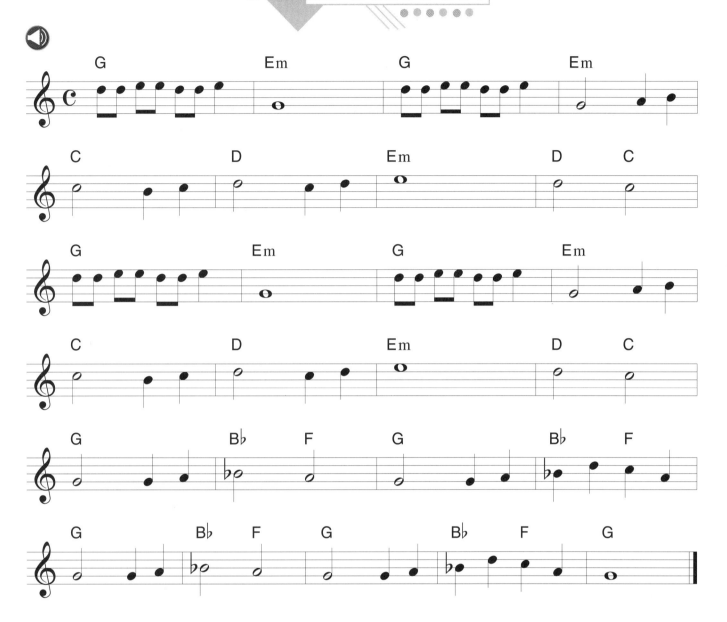

GRADUATION

Notes

Fact File

RESTS

An important part of music is what you DON'T play.
Rests tell you to be silent for a certain period of time during a measure.

WHOLE REST	4 BEATS OF SILENCE	▬
HALF REST	2 BEATS OF SILENCE	▬
QUARTER REST	1 BEAT OF SILENCE	𝄽
EIGHTH REST	1/2 BEAT OF SILENCE	𝄾

WHOLE   HALF   QUARTER   EIGHTH

1 2 3 4   1 2 **3** 4   **1** 2 **3** 4   1 & 2 & 3 & 4 &

GEOLOGY

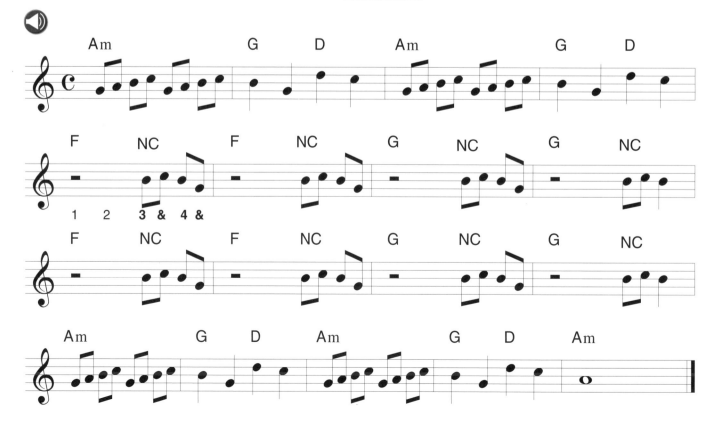

A TALE OF TWO SCALES

The notes on the first 3 strings with (B) make the scale called "G Mixolydian".

Now with (B♭)   This scale is called "G Dorian".

Play these scales as quickly, smoothly and evenly as possible.
This will make it easier to memorize and play all of your songs.

Fact File

* REPEAT SIGNS: ||:   :||

The section of music between two repeat signs is played twice, unless instructions are given to play more than twice (3x) (4x). If there is no repeat sign at the front of a section, go all the way back to the beginning of the song.

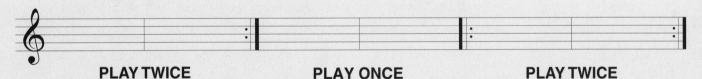

PLAY TWICE   **PLAY ONCE**   **PLAY TWICE**

The **fermata** (or hold sign) ⌢ indicates that there is a pause in time for the note below.

...land _____   of   the   free,   and   the...

Many songs end with a fermata on the last note. Go back and add a fermata to any of the previous songs that sound as though the last note should be held longer than its actual value.

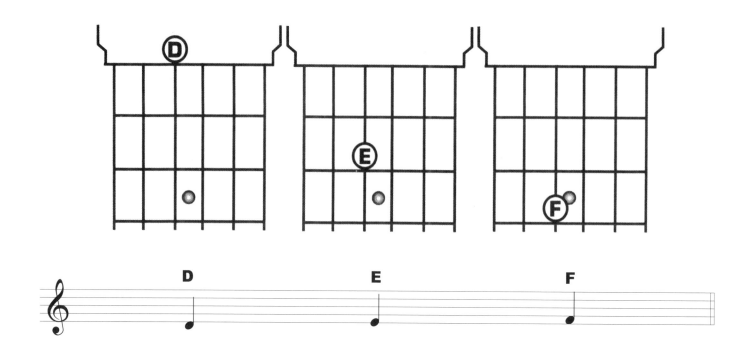

To play D: Pluck the 4th string open.
To play E: Place the 2nd finger on the 2nd fret of this string.
To play F: Place the 3rd finger on the 3rd fret of this string.

FORTHRIGHT?

DELIVERY

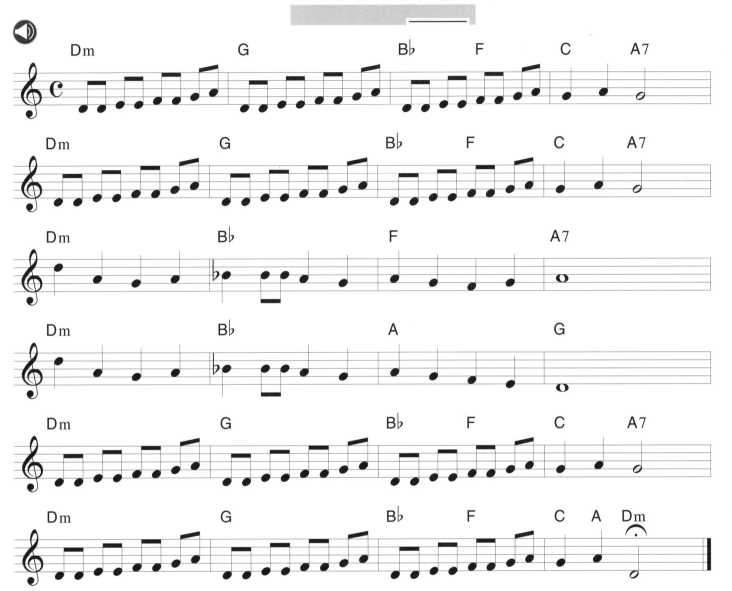

Fact File

COMING UP:

PICK- UP NOTES

Not every song starts with beat 1 of the first measure.
Pick- up notes are one or more notes that start a song
before the first full measure.

"This land is   your   land"

2   3   4 | 1   2   3   4
(pick-up notes)

Fact File

THE TIE

When a note needs to ring longer than the rest of a measure, a **tie** is used. The note on the other end of the tie is not played.

1 2 3 4   1 2 **3 4**

STAIRCASE

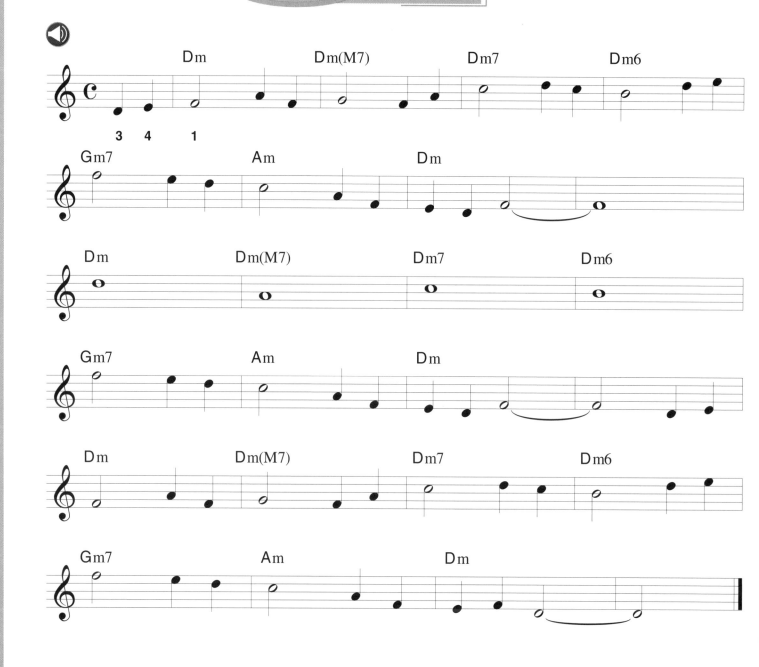

PENTATONIC

Fact File

COMING UP:

LEDGER LINES

Short lines added above or below the staff for higher or lower notes

E F G A B C...   F E D C B A...

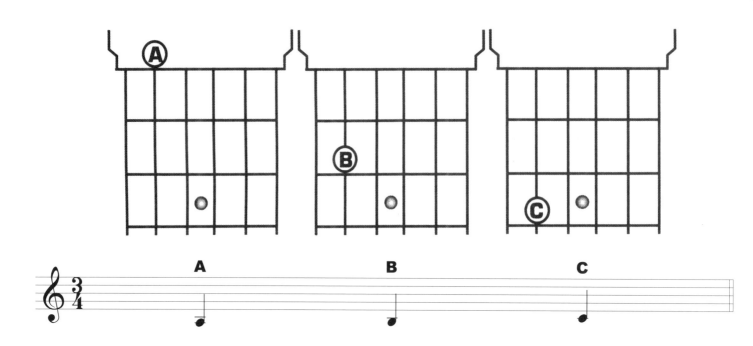

To play A: Pluck the 5th string open.
To play B: Place the 2nd finger on the 2nd fret of this string.
To play C: Place the 3rd finger on the 3rd fret of this string.

ADRIAN

OUT ON A LEDGER

Notes

5TH WHEEL

Notes

A MINOR SETBACK

HIGH A (ON THE 1ST STRING)

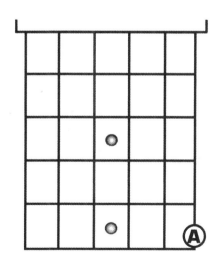

To play A: Place the 4th finger on the 5th fret of the 1st string.

The **A minor** scale:

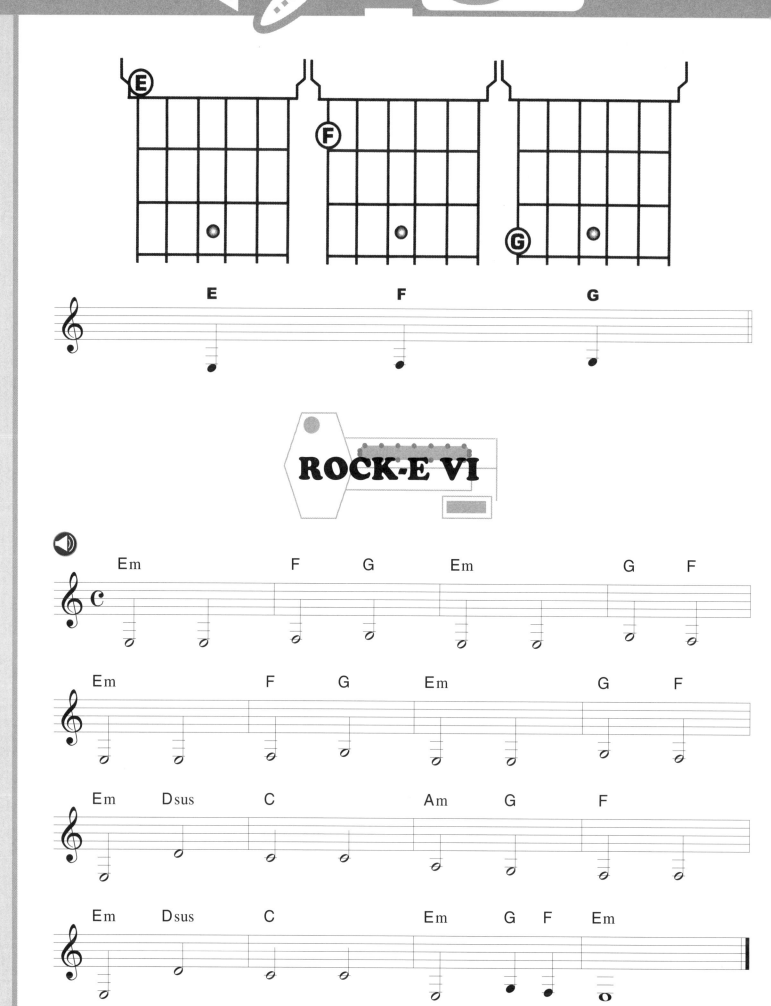

SURF STRING

OCTAVEE

Fact File

18 NOTE REVIEW

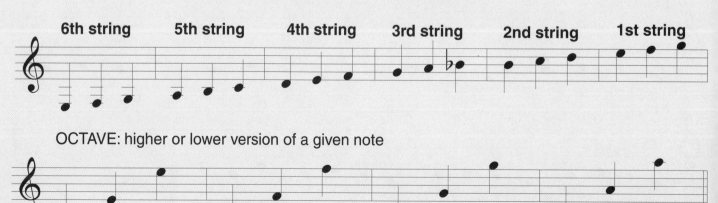

OCTAVE: higher or lower version of a given note

UPSHOT

Congratulations!
You're Ready!

Notes